Advances in Alchemy

Five Startling Stories of Chemistry and Biology

Nury Vittachi
Illustrations by Step Cheung

Contents

The Strange Adventures of Doctor Poison
F. F. Runge

The Young Woman Who Was Forgotten
Rosalind Franklin

The Girl in the Chamber of Corpses
Alessandra Giliani

The Farm Girl Who Made Your Milk Safe
Alice Evans

A Tasty Treat Found by Accident
Frank Epperson

STEP C.

THE STRANGE ADVENTURES OF DR. POiSON

OOPS! A BOY AGED 15 accidentally squirted poison into his eye. Uh-oh! This seemed like very bad news.

The young man's name was Friedleib Ferdinand Runge, but that was hard to remember — so most people just called him F. F.

F. F. was helping his uncle in the laboratory, and was handling a plant called henbane. Henbane has nothing to do with chickens, but comes from ancient words meaning "deadly poison".

He was trying to get the juice out of the plant when a bit of it squirted into his eye.

Good news: Not much went in, and he suffered no lasting damage.

But the even better news was that the boy, F. F., reacted like a scientist. He was fascinated. He wanted to record the data.

So he raced to a mirror and discovered that the little black disk in the middle of his eye had suddenly grown large.

Then it gradually shrank back to the same size as the one in the other eye. Remarkable!

Friedlieb was born in Germany in 1794. After working with his uncle and having his happy accident he became a scientist (although there was no such word in those days, as the word "scientist" was coined in 1832).

When F. F. was 25, he was quite well known at his university as a master of chemical analysis. His nickname was Doctor Poison, because he was fearless about doing experiments with chemicals that other people were scared of.

Living in the area was a very famous writer named Johann Wolfgang von Goethe, one of Europe's top literary celebrities.

Goethe wanted to meet Dr. Poison.

F. F. Runge, who was very poor, borrowed a smart black hat and a frock coat, and took his cat with him, too.

He told Goethe all about how chemicals worked, and even put a drop of a chemical in the eye of his cat, to show how the pupil would grow large. (It didn't hurt the cat.)

Goethe was amazed.

He handed F. F. a little bag of beans which had been sent to him from Greece. People used the beans to make a marvelous drink called mocha coffee.

He gave the young man a challenge:
What are the chemicals in this?

F. F. took the beans back to his lab and worked on them. He deduced that that the chemical that made coffee so popular was a white crystalline substance hidden inside.
He was right. We now call that chemical caffeine.

F. F. Runge also developed paper chromatography, which is when you use a strip of paper which changes color to tell you important details about a liquid. This is used in pregnancy tests and has many other uses.

When F. F. died, he was no longer called Dr. Poison. The newspaper announcement said: "After a brief illness, Dr. Friedlieb Ferdinand Runge, Professor of Technology, died this morning at six o'clock in his 74th year."

If your parents like to drink coffee, perhaps you can tell them about F. F., who went from being Dr. Poison to being Professor of Technology, and who discovered caffeine on the way.

THE YOUNG WOMAN WHO WAS FORGOTTEN

SCIENTISTS DISCOVERED THAT PEOPLE contain secret plans — instructions on how to build a human. It sounds strange, doesn't it, like a movie plot?

But it's true. Every cell in the human body contains molecules called DNA, which hold the information needed to make a person.

The full name of DNA is Deoxyribonucleic Acid, but that's hard to spell or say, even for scientists. So we all just say DNA.

Who discovered this? Quite a few people, but let's look at one of the contributors.

In 1950, Rosalind Franklin was 29 years old, and got a job working as a scientific researcher at a university laboratory in the UK.

She was clever, but some people found her to be rather a grumpy person, and she definitely had a sharp tongue.

She worked with a man called Maurice Wilkins, who was the opposite: shy, polite and friendly. Sometimes people who are opposites fit together well, but not in this case. The two did not get on.

By 1953, scientists all knew that DNA existed, but nobody had ever seen it. It became a race to see who could find it first. (It was not a real race, of course, but scientists can be competitive, and they all wanted the glory of being the first to find something, and thus achieve fame.)

At that time, Rosalind and Maurice were part of a team led by two highly esteemed scientists, James Watson and Francis Crick.

One day, Rosalind organized for one of her students (she worked at a university) to use special cameras to try to take pictures of DNA.

This technique had never worked before. But this time, the result was a picture which was a rather fuzzy image with an odd shape in it. It was listed simply as "Photograph 51". The student took the picture with him to the office of the other scientist (the friendly one), Maurice Wilkins.

Then one of the project leaders, top scientist James Watson, came to Rosalind's room and warned that other scientists were close to finding the answer. He said that this team urgently needed to recheck their results if they were to have a chance of winning the race.

STEP C.

It seems that Rosalind may have thought that he was implying that she don't know how to interpret her own data. Anyway, whatever she thought, the result was that she shouted at him!

Watson backed out of the room — and bumped straight into shy Maurice Wilkins, who had come to see what the noise was about.

Quiet, friendly Wilkins took Watson to his room and showed him Photograph 51.

The two top scientists, Watson and Crick, examined it carefully and worked out that DNA was a very odd molecule, like two ladders braided together. They filled in all the details and published their results.

The two men became very famous and won the Nobel Prize.

Rosalind was forgotten. After her death, people discovered that it was her research which led to the taking of the all-important Photograph 51. Had she been left out of the official reports because she was female? Or because she was hard to get along with? Or because her contribution had been quite small?

People have debated these issues for a long time (and will surely continue to do so), but here we'll make no judgment, and take just one lesson from this incident.

It's always worth being friendly and likeable! Science is a team game, and being cooperative is really helpful.

THE GIRL IN THE CHAMBER OF CORPSES

PEOPLE WERE SCARED OF the natural philosopher and his chief assistant, despite the fact that he was a doctor and she was little more than a child.

That was because the expertise of Dr Mondino de' Liuzzi and his young assistant Alessandra Giliani was cutting up dead bodies in the name of science.

People did not want to visit the place where they worked, because they worried that evil spirits lurked there.

This fear made good scientific sense. Dead bodies soon rotted and if you touched them, you could easily get sick and die of invisible evil spirits, which we would now call infectious viruses and bacteria.

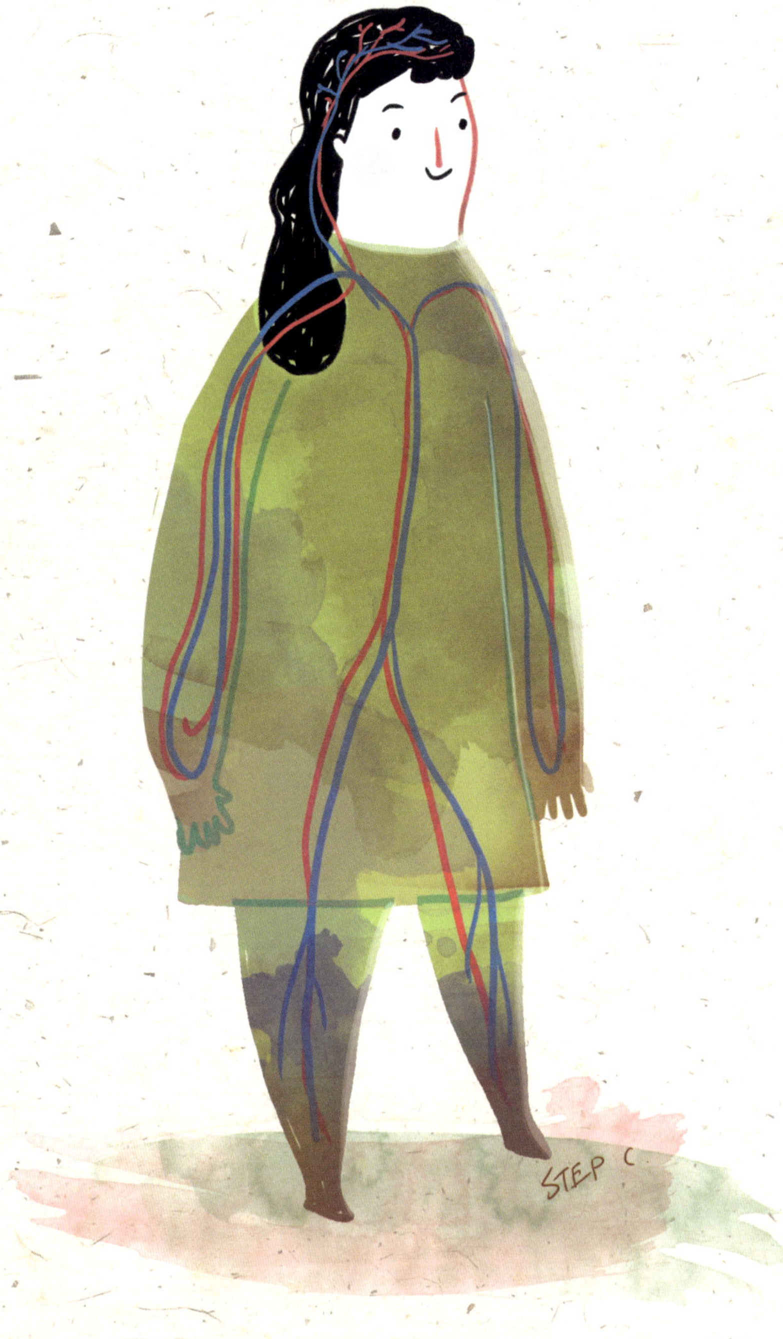
STEP C

Alessandra prepared corpses for demonstrations and Dr de' Liuzzi would show audiences the internal organs of humans, explaining what they did.

The pair were creative, too.

Dr de' Liuzzi had an amazing way of stitching together two thin pieces of human tissue. He would hold the flaps of skin together and get a large ant to bite them!

Then he would kill the ant but leave the ant's head in place. He could stitch a wound together with a row of ants' heads.

Alessandra, a teenager, had also invented a new medical technique.

She had found a way of draining blood from a fresh dead body and replacing it with a dark liquid dye. That meant that you could see where the blood flowed through the human body.

The scientist was quite successful and soon had a few other assistants. One of them, a young man named Otto, fell in love with Alessandra.

This happened in the early 1300s in Italy. The doctor wrote a book about all the parts of the human body and it became the most important book of anatomy for hundreds of years.

But what happened to Alessandra?

By the time she was 19, she and Otto had decided to get married.

But then one day, after coming home from work, the young woman felt sick — very sick.

Alessandra had probably picked up an infection from one of the dead bodies. Today we have medicines called "antibiotics" to halt dangerous infections, but in those days poor Otto could do nothing.

Alessandra died. It is believed that Otto put her remains in a pot and put a plaque on it, saying: "In this urn, awaiting the Resurrection, are the mortal remains of Alessandra Giliani, young woman of Persiceto, adept at anatomical demonstrations and unequalled disciple of the most famous doctor, Mondino de' Liuzzi."

There's not much information about her, so the details of her life come from guesswork.

But if she lived as we believe, then, 700 years ago, she gave her life to increase medical knowledge.

And today, if you get sick, related medical knowledge will make you well again. Maybe say a quick thank you to Alessandra, in case she is looking down on us!

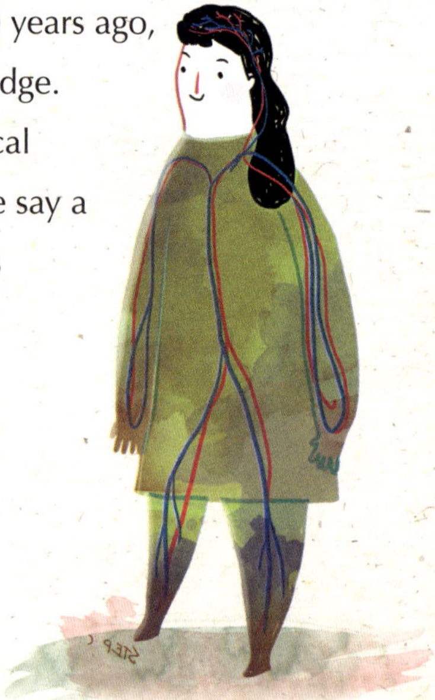

THE FARM GIRL WHO MADE YOUR MILK SAFE

A FARM GIRL called Alice had a problem. She wanted to change the world, to make a difference, to leave her mark on humanity.

But what hope was there? She was a farm girl. And a poor one, at that.

Worse still, she wasn't even healthy — as a small child, she and her brother contracted a bad disease called scarlet fever, and only narrowly survived.

Alice Catherine Evans lived on a small farm in the countryside in Pennsylvania in the USA. Her parents did not earn enough money to send her to university, and besides, in those days, the late 1800s, girls were rarely encouraged to study.

When she left school, she took the only option available to her, becoming a teacher in a small town nearby.

Then one day, she heard that a famous university called Cornell University was offering free classes to poor rural teachers.

She signed up and was soon studying bacteria, which many scientists believed were the cause of diseases like the one she had survived.

But it seemed that she could never escape her farming background.

When she graduated and got a job, it was as a research scientist serving the dairy farm industry. Her assignment was to improve the flavor of cheese.

One day, when she was in her early 30s, she had a thought, putting together the things she knew about farms, bacteria and disease. There were several mystery illnesses that humans had — could it be that they came from bacteria that caused diseases that people thought only cows got?

She went to her papers to take a look, and did some fresh research. Her studies showed a connection.

She tried to tell people with power about this. But they didn't listen: she was a woman, and they thought she didn't have enough qualifications to count as a real scientist. But a science journal published her claim in 1918.

STEP C.

Over the next few years, it became clear that she was right. Male scientists discovered the same thing — and plans were put in place to see what should be done.

Scientists knew that if you heated milk in a certain way, you would kill all the germs in it while keeping the goodness of the milk unchanged. This was called Pasteurization, after the man who discovered it, Louis Pasteur.

Scientists used Alice Evans' findings to make a case for all milk to be processed in this way.

Today, if you go to your local store, whether it is in Singapore, or New York, or Nairobi, you will almost definitely find words such as "Pasteurized" printed in small letters on the carton. And you can drink it knowing that it will do you no harm.

And it's all because a farm girl called Alice, who wanted to make a difference in the world, succeeded in doing just that. In every area of interest, there are discoveries to be made. So, what are you interested in?

A TASTY TREAT FOUND BY ACCIDENT

DO YOU LOVE FROZEN SNACKS? Most young people love popsicles, also known as ice lollies or ice pops.

These are pieces of fruit-flavored sugar-ice on a stick, sometimes with multi-colored sections or sweet bits added.

Most foods these days are invented by chefs working in kitchens belonging to restaurants or to big corporations. But in the past, foods were invented by ordinary people.

Frank Epperson was only about 11 years old when he accidentally invented popsicles, in 1905. In those days, the only frozen dessert known to most people was ice cream.

Frank wasn't trying to make a dessert, or any type of food. He was just thirsty. You couldn't buy a carton of real juice then — if you wanted a sweet drink, you bought oranges and squeezed them. If you could not afford to do that, you stirred fruit-flavored powder into a glass of tap water.

One cold night, the boy was stirring such a drink when he stepped out of the house, and put the glass down for a moment.

But then he forgot all about it and went inside and put himself to bed without thinking about his drink.

The next morning he stepped outside and found that the drink had frozen solid. He pulled the stirring stick upwards and the drink came with it — it kept its shape, looking like a huge, brightly colored ice-cube. Out of curiosity, he licked it and found it tasted good.

And then he forgot all about it.

Seventeen years later it popped back into his mind. He was helping to cater for a firemen's ball in his home city, which was Oakland, in California, in the USA.

He made a large batch of frozen drinks to lick and served them to the party-goers, who loved them. The following year, he sold the "frozen lollipops" as snacks at an amusment park, and realized that this was a good idea for a business. They were cheap and easy to make, and quite profitable. They were just made from tap water and a bit of sweetened, fruit-flavored powder.

In 1923, Frank Epperson took out a patent, which is a document certifying that you have invented something new, and started selling them.

He wanted to call them epsicles, but he had children of his own then, and they preferred the name popsicles. Their choice stuck, especially when a New York company started mass-producing them under that name. One of the meanings of the word "pop" is "sweet drink" and the other part of the word comes from "icicle".

These days you can buy popsicles (or ice lollies) all over the world in flavors of fruit or chocolate or even green tea.

One of the reasons children love them so much is that they often change the color of your tongue for a while. Eat a blue popsicle and then stick your tongue out in front of a mirror — it's a pretty funny sight!

KEEP READING

READING ABOUT THE LIVES of scientists and other discoverers adds to our store of knowledge, but we hope also leads us towards something much greater, which is wisdom.

This book is part of a series, which we hope you'll enjoy reading, and will spur you on to do your own scientific research.

The creators of this book wish you success in your explorations.

THE YOUNG SCIENTISTS SERIES

Book 1: SECRETS IN THE ROCKS
Five Astounding Tales of People Solving Mysteries Beneath Our Feet

Book 2: FABULOUS PHYSICS
Five Amazing Stories of People Who Solved Nature's Puzzles

Book 3: MAGICAL MATHEMATICS
Five Astonishing Stories of People Who Did Miracles with Numbers

Book 4: BREAKERS OF BARRIERS
Five Stunning Stories of People Demolishing Walls to Make History

Book 5: SCIENTIFIC PIONEERS
Five Incredible Tales of People Who Helped Develop the Scientific Method

Book 6: THE AMAZING QUANTUM
Five Awesome Stories of People Who Made a Revolution in Physics

Book 7: THE SCIENCE OF HUMANITY
Five Fascinating Stories of People Who Helped Us Understand Ourselves

Book 8: WOMEN OF DISCOVERY
Five Super Stories of Fabulous Females Who Made Scientific History

Book 9: THE INVENTOR'S SPARK
Five Marvelous Stories of People Who Helped Shape the Modern World

Book 10: ADVANCES IN ALCHEMY
Five Startling Stories of Chemistry and Biology

Book 11: THE CALL OF THE STARS
Five Wonderful Stories of People Looking to the Heavens

Book 12: MYSTERIES OF NATURE'S LAWS
Five Striking Stories of People Investigating the Deepest Puzzles of Reality

Published by

WS Education, an imprint of
World Scientific Publishing Co. Pte. Ltd.
5 Toh Tuck Link, Singapore 596224
USA office: 27 Warren Street, Suite 401-402, Hackensack, NJ 07601
UK office: 57 Shelton Street, Covent Garden, London WC2H 9HE

National Library Board, Singapore Cataloguing in Publication Data
Name(s): Vittachi, Nury, 1958– | Cheung, Step, illustrator.
Title: Advances in alchemy : five startling stories of chemistry and biology / author, Nury Vittachi ; illustrator, Step Cheung.
Other title(s): Young scientists series ; 10.
Description: Singapore : World Scientific Publishing Co Pte Ltd, 2017.
Identifier(s): OCN 969708634 | ISBN 978-981-3221-68-0 (paperback)
Subject(s): LCSH: Chemists--Juvenile literature. | Biologists--Juvenile literature. | Scientists--Juvenile literature. | Chemistry--Juvenile literature. | Biology--Juvenile literature. | Science--Juvenile literature.
Classification: DDC 540.922--dc23

British Library Cataloguing-in-Publication Data
A catalogue record for this book is available from the British Library.

All royalties received will be channelled to the National Book Development Council of Singapore (NBDCS) as a gift from the author.

First published 2017
Reprinted 2018

Printed in Singapore